The memoirs of life

Surabhi Anand

BookLeaf Publishing

India | USA | UK

Presentation by *BookLeaf Publishing*

Web: www.bookleafpub.com

E-mail: info@bookleafpub.com

ISBN: 9789363314795

First edition 2024

Dedicated to my two little flowers:- Sparsh and
Sayansh.

ACKNOWLEDGEMENT

I would like to thank Bookleaf Publishing for this wonderful opportunity to share my work with the rest of the world and also my super awesome family (Esp my husband) who always supported me in working towards every crazy idea I had!!

PREFACE

A poetry is an outcome of tons of thoughts erased, nights of sleep lost, finding motivation at the strangest of places to weave the most wondeful basket of emotions to be read.

A Little Boat of Friendship

A small little boat of friendship and love,
Floating in the ocean of betrayal and pain.
Afraid to anchor, lest it be pulled down,
Charting its course through trecherous rains.

It navigates silently under a blanket of stars,
Sad memories to erase, fond ones to keep.
As ocean orchestrates a song with the waves,
The little boat gets rocked gently to sleep.

It came a long way, in search of a true friend,
Coz friends my dear are like threads of a strand.
Some lose warmth like the setting sun on a sea,
While others set loose like the grains of sand.

It floated tirelessly till the ends of the world,
Moments of laughter, forgotten and long gone.
No twisting of tales or stitching of new thoughts
,
No gatherings of dusk, nor the giggles of dawn.

One day nature spun the wheels of time,
And the ocean engulfed the boat's emptiness,
When a sight so lovely the boat's eyes beheld,
It wiped away all the memories of loneliness.

A Dance with Nature

The view was spectacular from the top of the
mountains,
It looked like a painting of the most beautiful
sorts,
The backdrop of clouds reflected in the streams,
Tranquil gusts of wind playing soft musical
notes.

I take off my boots to walk barefoot on the
ground,
The grass is drenched with the fresh morning
dew,
Every piece of land, revealing stories of its
wanderers,
Some who got lost, others discovered
themselves anew.

The heavenly blue sky gazing widely in my
eyes,
Stirring the undivulged secrets of my soul,
Placid water running deep in the gorges,
Glistening in the sun like diamonds shining
whole.

Blooming flowers caress forgotten touch of the
bees,
The dandelions burst into millions of wonders,
Raindrops spread sweet aroma of the Earth,
Grey sky clicking pictures with flashes of
thunder.

It rumbled as if it was a concert of the clouds,
The leaves on the trees swayed to thumping
beats,
I soaked in the drizzling confetti of the sky,
While losing my senses to this perpetual treat.

The raindrops carve tender paths on my face,
I dance to the unheard melodies of the land,
The mountain range sets a magnificent stage,
Blending with nature's performance so grand.

Your Reflection in my Heart

A fleeting glimpse of your visage,
My heart skipped a thousand beats,
The hands of clocks froze in time,
When accidentally our sights meet.

A fresh delicate garland of hope and trust,
Spreads its fragrance from your eyes to mine,
Resting over the promises of tomorrow,
Holding strong like a bridge in rain or shine.

Beauty was held in the beholder's eyes,
And wanderings were all certainly lost,
All that glittered had turned into gold,
The moment pathways of our lives crossed.

Like a Seagull, I glided over the ocean,
With strong and powerful lift of the wind,
Fluttering like a butterfly over the meadows,
My heart soaring high, could not be pinned.

The attraction was like an exponential storm,
Two magnets bridging along uncharted lands,
I waded through the complex forest of emotions,
Holding this fragile thread dearly in my hands.

I am so frightened to release you now,
Lest the ways of the world might pull us apart,
Just hold on to my gaze, a tad bit longer,
Until I have carved your reflection in my heart.

A Piece of Scrap Paper

I picked up my gel pen and a piece of scrap
paper,
The task was to list down grocery for stocking
days,
To recollect the items, I stared off the window,
But all I could see was the early morning haze.

My senses got wrapped by an envelope of
clouds,
And my mind wandered off to routes
unexplored,
Surrounded by a labyrinth of peculiar feelings,
Stallions of thoughts burst through close-fitting
doors.

Finding their way through the forgotten streets,
The voyage was a plethora of profound joy,
Germinating like saplings on the harshest of
lands,
Parading forward like a battleship's convoy.

The ink trickled through, like a silent mountain
stream,
Embellishing the paper with its exquisite allure,

Flowing with the smoothness of a mountain
zephyr,
Like a fairy's touch, so gentle and pure.

It formed a charming necklace of words,
Each word an emotion, strung piece by piece,
Giving birth to a saga of loveliest of proses,
Covering the paper's every wrinkle and crease.

The Giant Oak tree

Standing amidst the vibrant green fields,
Was a giant, weathered and tanned Oak tree,
It stood magnificently on its sturdy roots,
Laden with greenery never before seen.

Its history went back to the birth of the fields,
From sowing of seeds to the reaping of crops,
It passed through cycles of unusual seasons,
Stored in its bosom, pleasing scenes at the top.

Its dense canopy resembles a humongous
umbrella,
Spreading its shade through hot summer days,
Pockets in its trunk were home to little fauna,
The crisscross branches bear a playful maze.

A wonderful place to gather with comrades,
Sharing laughter of today, dreams of tomorrow,
Newborn threads binding love in the hearts,
Careless whispers being steered in
wheelbarrows.

Then life turned its pages in the course of time,
Folks ventured gradually into unknown terrains,
The great Oak tree stood alone by the field,
Waiting to feel the joyousness once again.

A Castle on the Rocks

Night was pitch black like deep mounds of coal,
The sky was inky like the darkest of chalks,
An endless mist loomed on shadows so eerie,
Illuminating the essence of the Castle on the
rocks.

Its silhouette cut against the night like a sword,
The scrapes on parapet display tales of combat,
Small saplings of life peering out of the rocks,
Fate sealed with isolation, no tangible contact.

It was accustomed to being a bountiful kingdom,
Hallways echoing with glorious folklores,
The beaming proud faces of the kins and kinds,
Spreading hopes and dreams and feelings amore.

Markets overflowed with well-crafted metals,
Channels of trades opened and thrived,
Merchants and traders travelled the world,
And brought exquisite gifts as they arrived.

The flames of fanfare extinguished in time,
As trumpets of war resonated nearby,
The flags were tied and fastened in strings,
And natives were compelled to bid goodbye.

Now all that remains is a structure in horizon,
Like a souvenir rusted with the passage of time,
A legend all chained up in memories of glory,
Casting dark shadows on its days of prime.

Here comes Spring!

Here comes Spring, with bountiful of colors,
Carpet of fresh grass as smooth as butter.
Fresh breeze relays the scent of flowers,
Bells are chiming in the tall clock towers.

Bunch of little florets, pink, yellow and blue,
Like shop full of candies, for me and for you.
Trees grow cover with bunches of fresh leaves,
Nature's enchantment is so hard to believe!

Butterflies flutter spreading powdery wing dust,
Consuming the sweetness of flowers with lust.
The birds tweet songs of home and migration,
Celebrating the nature's special coronation.

A shiny half rainbow adds splendor to the scene,
Shimmering like treasures under the Sun's sheen.
The valley transformed into a peaceful retreat,
Carried away on water like frozen ice sheet.

A flood of sensations, purposeful and pure,
To realize its depth, I was too immature.
My heart broke free from the worldly traps,
Happiness was truly in mother nature's lap.

Our Feathered Friends

Soaring in the sky and perching on tall trees,
Playful wings are quick to catch the breeze,
Songbirds and sparrows are filled with joy,
An exhibit of symmetry, truly to enjoy.

Vibrant plumage is dazzling to the eyes,
The darting and take-off, leaves us mesmerized.
From flights of Robin to mighty Eagle's dive,
Each flock of birds looks naturally specialized.

In the midst of dawn, their chirps reverberate,
Welcoming the mornings as if to celebrate.
Nesting in the branches is their safe haven,
Crafted beautifully like a world-class mason.

Alight on the topmost branch or set in an aerial
dance,
These birds of feathers, always put us in a
trance.
Let's cherish the company of each feathered
friend,
As they are connecting the world from end to
end.

A Camping Night

The stars shone down like small twinkling
lights,
While cluster of fireflies blinked in April skies,
A serene night that was as quiet as a mouse,
We were busy unpacking our camping supplies.

These small flying lanterns lit up the jungle
trails,
Casting magic as they buzzed in leaps and
bounds,
Like beacon of lighthouses revolving tirelessly,
They flew in patterns without making a sound.

The world was beautiful in its quiet and calm,
Like the mesmerizing peace before a wicked
storm,
We wrapped ourselves in our cozy blankets,
Sipping on some hot tea to keep ourselves warm.

Aroma of grilled veggies was a delectable treat,
Hanging in the air like a bunch of helium
balloons,
Beer steins overflowed with drinks and stories,
As thunderclouds crept slowly covering the
moon.

The rumbling was intermittent like playing slow
drums,
It seemed to coincide with a giant gnome's grunt,
The rain drops began to quench the thirsty fire,
As tents stood confidently bearing the storm's
brunt.

We all rejoiced in this momentous performance,
Seeking nature's thrills from the refuge of a tent,
For once comes daylight, all transforms into a
dream,
That would look like something never to be
meant.

Colors of a Rainbow

Radiance of colors in a spectrum of divine,
Shining brightly, nature's best designs.

Red looks fiery that leads the way,
Kindling the sky with its lively play.

Orange spreads warmth while bringing delight,
Blending coherently with the sky's natural light.

Yellow color shows a cheerful sunflower field,
Brightening the world with its gleaming yield.

Green is the color of shades of life and growth,
Bearing the Earth with its fertile oath.

Blue- spreads vast, calming the expanse above,
Nurturing the soul with its peaceful love.

Indigo depicts a brooding profound hue,
Introspecting a new thoughtful view.

Violet is the majestic and mysterious tone,
Bounding the rainbow in a beauty of its own.

A union of colors painted in perfect harmony,

Carving an infinite rainbow in nature's
symphony.

The Lost Love

Strings of the heart once intertwined,
Resonance of love that was fully sublime.
Memories lingered in an intense refrain,
Of the one whom I'll never hold again.

Tattered pages of a book never told,
Memories faded but the ache was untold.
Silently, I yearn for your gentle embrace,
The warmth of your hands, the smile on your
face.

Nights I would spend staring out at the stars,
Wondering if you could hear my voice that far.
The space between us is like an endless sea,
It locks me in its depth, never setting me free.

If only I could turn back the hands of time,
Recapturing the memories of our prime.
I am now lonely and entirely heart broken,
Until the ends of time, your love in me is frozen.

A Land of Mysteries

A beautiful castle from the tales of the fairies,
Surrounded by the most gorgeous of falls,
Gardens so flowery and full of lush greens,
Fruit laden trees that surrounded the walls.

The garden appeared like a palette of colors,
Decorated with a range of the prettiest of pots,
The neighborhood carried wonderful fragrances,
Like bottles of rare perfumes, poured in lots.

Windows are glistening with shimmering rays,
Their brightness reflecting until the clouds,
The turrets stand tall like Californian Red
Woods,
Casting their shadows on the fortress all around.

The unfurled flags tell stories of triumph,
Bright banners decorate the fort's barricades,
The golden statues of kings and noble steeds,
Exhibit the kingdom's glory and accolades.

A picture so perfect as if it were a dream,
Delicate images sown into a tapestry,
A world that appeared too alluring to be real,
Driving the spectators to a land of mysteries.

Mighty Waterfall

Thunderous rapids, flowing since eternity,
Over jagged cliffs, the flow begins its descent,
Cascading downhills with vigorous energy,
Burbling through clouds evidently heaven-sent.

Torrential waters falling and tumbling loose,
Carving through the landscape a destined path,
Mist mesmerizing the air with its embrace,
Refracting light into a shimmering Persian bath.

Relentless waters generate thunderous sounds,
Currents and whirlpools make swirling designs,
Onlookers bewitched by its majestic essence,
Its aura appeared to be angelic and divine.

Rushing rivers feed the watery display,
A testament to nature's unbridled might,
Sustaining flora that grows day and night,
This mighty waterfall is a wonderful delight.

The Majestic Elephant

Mighty Monarchs of the prairie lands,
Whose shadow towers above the rest,
Wrinkled skin bears the grunts of time,
Little crown of hair, decorating its crest.

The mighty trunk snakes around its food,
Big thumping feets, shudder the ground,
Deep eyes portray a sensitive soul,
Ears spread like sails, flapping around.

A gentle giant, adorned with ornaments,
To match its grandeur at an Indian wedding,
Epic and gallant in its righteous state,
Maneuvering meticulously in its treading.

A humble creature borne by mother nature,
Tutoring the lessons of kindness and hope,
Nimble and naughty in their disposition,
Actions form images like kaleidoscopes.

Guardians of nature, forging new trails,
Enriching the Earth until the very end,
The majestic elephants are nature's treasures,
That we must love, protect and defend.

The Colorful Umbrella

I spotted a vendor down the street,
What a colorful umbrella he owned!
It had a mix of beautiful patterns,
Like vibrant fishes in a pond.

The printed bright blue circles,
Felt like fresh drops of rain,
A dash of yellow in between,
Reminded me of cornfield plains.

Little red hearts arranged on the cloth,
Were like soldiers of Queen of Hearts,
Bands of green spread out in rows,
Gave the sense of an abstract art.

The border was the most exquisite,
Decorated with fluffy pink frills,
It resembled a child's ballet dress,
Watching it twirl, was such a thrill!

It swept me to the land of marshmallows,
And never ending crush of candies,
The glorious magnificent umbrella I see,
Gives this hawker the looks of a dandy!

What is Poetry?

What is poetry, this enigmatic art,
That dances with words, and speaks to the heart?
It is not merely lines, or a structured rhyme,
But a tapestry of emotions, a symphony sublime.

Poetry is the language of the soul,
A vehicle to express what words can't control.
It paints with metaphors, weaves images so
clear,
That they evoke emotions, joy or a silent tear.

In the verses, a mirror of the human experience,
Reflections of love, loss, and the search for
significance.
Poetry gives voice to the unspoken thoughts,
Unveiling the depths that our minds have
wrought.

It is not bound by rules, nor constrained by form,
Poetry flows freely, like a gentle storm.
From the simplest haiku to the grandest of odes,
Each line a stepping stone, leading down
untrodden roads.

Poetry is the symphony of the written word,

Where each stanza is a note, a melody heard.
It is the dance of language, the rhythm of life,
Capturing the essence of our joys and our strife.

So what is poetry, this enchanting art?
It is the bridge between the mind and the heart.
It is the voice that speaks when words fail to
convey,
The timeless expression of the human way.

Being Human

To be human, a complex tapestry unfurled,
A blend of emotions, thoughts that swirl.
Joy and sorrow, laughter and tears,
Traversing a spectrum of hopes and fears.

We are dreamers, reaching for the stars above,
Seeking answers, craving knowledge, and
yearning for love.
Endowed with the power to create and to
destroy,
Our actions and choices, a constant source of
employ.

Vulnerability, our greatest strength and our flaw,
Exposing our hearts, our spirits to the world's
awe.
Yet, it is in this fragility that we find our true
might,
Overcoming obstacles, standing tall in the face
of life's plight.

To be human is to feel deeply, to empathize and
to care,
To embrace our flaws, our triumphs, and our
despair.

It is to seek purpose, to find meaning in every
breath,
To dance with the rhythm of life, from birth to
death.

We are complex beings, with the capacity to
grow and learn,
To make mistakes, to stumble, and then patiently
to discern.
For it is in our humanity that we find the path to
transcend,
Unlocking the potential that lies within, waiting
to ascend.

So let us celebrate this gift of being human, this
miraculous state,
Embracing the journey, the challenges, the joys
that await.
For in our shared experience, we find a common
thread,
That binds us together, now and long after we're
dead.

Baby in my Arms

The nights were nonchalant, untamed and dozy,
While mornings were full of tasks and workouts,
Friends were the spiciest ingredients of life,
The year was filled with Staycations throughout.

Erratic schedules spawning arbitrary plans,
From poker to pool parties or horse - riding
farms,
Change was the only eternal state,
Until I held a little baby in my arms.

My tasks in a day were uncomplicated,
All my possessions were neatly stockpiled,
Books and papers supplemented the library,
Budding flowers decorated the porch and aisles.

No bins of medicines or bittersweet syrups,
No band-aids for bruises or pain relief balms,
Change was the only eternal state,
Until I held a little baby in my arms.

I was a bit foolhardy, reckless and naive,
Not caring whether I was right or wrong,
"I can always try to do it again",
Was my go-to mantra & comeback song.

No trepidation of someone being injured,
Or dealing with broken emergency alarms,
Change was the only eternal state,
Until I held a little baby in my arms.

The days roll by like flashes of lightening,
And nights to me no longer belong,
As I am almost on the brink of despairing,
These tiny little fingers grasp me strong.

Never did I feel a love so compelling,
A powerful hurricane like the eye of the storm,
Change was no longer an eternal state,
Ever since I held my baby in my arms.

Mending Broken Bonds

The bonds that once held us all strong,
Is lying broken, tattered and torn,
The path to mending seems very long, the
journey is forlorn.
Yet, in the gloominess of despair,
a slight glimmer of light remains,
A chance to sew back rift of torn bonds,
to soothe the lingering pains.

With patience and care, we must begin to sew,
The fragments of trust that have been rent so.
Stitching each piece, with a steadfast hand,
Weaving a tapestry, to help us understand.

The scars that remain may never fully fade,
But in their wake, a stronger bond can be made.
For it is through the struggle, the tears, and the
strife,
That we find the resilience to breathe new life.

Forgiveness, the salve that soothes the wounded
heart,
Allowing us to let go, to make a fresh start.
To see the other through eyes of compassion and
grace,

And find the courage to reclaim our rightful
place.

Together, we'll walk the path, step by cautious
step,
Rebuilding the trust that was so carelessly
bereft.
Brick by brick, we'll construct a foundation
anew,
Where the bonds we once shared, become
stronger and true.

Though the journey may be long, and the
challenges great,
The rewards of mending broken bonds, they
outweigh the wait.
For in the end, we'll stand, our spirits renewed
and whole,
Embracing the strength of a bond that can never
be untold.

www.ingramcontent.com/pod-product-compliance
Lightning Source LLC
LaVergne TN
LVHW010953200726
843509LV00013B/2406